seeing red

seeing red

Dennis Cooley

TURNSTONE PRESS

Turnstone Press
607-100 Arthur Street
Artspace Building
Winnipeg, MB
R3B 1H3 Canada
www.TurnstonePress.com

Turnstone Press gratefully acknowledges the assistance of The Canada
Council for the Arts, the Manitoba Arts Council, the Government of
Canada through the Book Publishing Industry Development Program and
the Government of Manitoba through the Department of Culture, Heritage
and Tourism, Arts Branch, for our publishing activities.

   Canadä

The Canada Council | Le Conseil des Arts
for the Arts | du Canada

MANITOBA arts COUNCIL
CONSEIL DES DU MANITOBA

Cover design: Tétro Design
Interior design: Sharon Caseburg
Printed and bound in Canada by Kromar Printing Ltd. for Turnstone Press.

Several of these poems are reprinted with permission from pachyderm
press, which in 1990 published a chapbook of Dennis Cooley's Dracula
poems, *burglar of blood*, and with permission from Anansi Press, which
published "crewel work" in 2000 in *Sunfall*, a book by Dennis Cooley.
The poems that are reprinted in *seeing red* are slightly revised.

National Library of Canada Cataloguing in Publication Data

Cooley, Dennis, 1944-
  Seeing red / Dennis Cooley.

  Poems.
  ISBN 0-88801-277-2

  I. Title.
PS8555.O575S43 2003   C811'.54   C2003-910479-6
PR9199.3.C642S43 2003

for the once-bitten

With thanks to those at Turnstone—Sharon Caseburg, Pat Sanders, Kelly Stifora, and Todd Besant—who have treated the text with exemplary patience and care. And with thanks to my family—Diane, Dana, and Megan— who have shown their own kinds of patience and care.

Contents

seeing red

open

yes when i spread
my hand like that
/it opens, the ink spreads
thats me i sniff slink across dreams you carry
nightmare from stiff arm to ankle it speeds
my cape scrapes darkness scoops it around
piles it up bigger and bigger
your niggling desires ink in

a cape carp carpe diem its all there
fish leather jacket your blue rain coat
it all sinks in me & my humerus
i play a hunch
radius ulna carpals metacarpals digits
you can count on that right to your final
archaeological fidget

Fledermaus man they call me you must have heard
i am making a come-back in Germany
the movie houses are fluttery with light
the hot buttery breath blows it up & out it goes
chauve souris bald mouse hot pulse i feed on

the effluvia of your fears
though at first it puzzles light
jerks in smokey St. Vitus dance

there's a moon out tonight

the moon
I can see
the moon looks
& looks

as if it's a face someone's pulled
a rake over & it's healed almost

I can see
in the dark
see in you
darkness roll up
carriage in a cloud
of dissolved sugar

it is red & it seeks
to get out it wants
to rain all over you
it wants to leave you
i don't want to leave you
soaked with desire

don't want to see you
, alone
, stuck
in the thick

blind in the heat in the blind heat in the blind

truly I saw, say:

you a tree, bleeding
& me sucking down leaves
thirsty as a koala
you could be cocacola

& then your body
one long bone
blood mists around
                    & in
singing clear as glass
                as alone

crewel work

embroidered our borders, our bodies
                        the deft need
      le point I bring
you in your parlour your pallor
you could be a lamp, shaded

                        no lady i feel no male
                        volence nor offer any
                  I always knew how you rose
                     that you would
                                    -rise ,silent as bread
                  deaf I thought at first you held
                  & inspected closely turned it
                  over & over were you astonished i could do
                        would do it at all
                        did you think how ill
                        bred it is a tall
                  man with needles & thread at the door

                  were you so bored it would
                  excite you perhaps it does not
                  matter I saw it bring a scarlet
                  kerchief to your face yes though
                  hand to throat, cheek, you tried to cover
                  your eyes the quick light, then away
                  what is in them what do you hide

                  there is a swish of skirts & you saying
                  come in come in you say, me at the door
                  tall shadow at your feet the clock
                  tock tock dock duck talking in the woodflesh

you stand on your soft soft shoes
the tendons stand out the boundary
we feel all over our faces come in
you say please won't you come in
teeter on the faint fragrance your body gives
the way you let it off, fruit from a bowl

say something why don't you say something

your world   I step into   is
not the crystal palace though it could be
lined with porcelain with a certain
uncertainty it could be a teapot i step inside

should I stop i should stop
sounds in your body quicken
the heat ticking the ticks between us
the air goes funny & tick tick tick
like that: an engine cooling
the anguish or injury you may do

                              oh do not
              put your fingers in
              the engines of your dreams

there is a smell in your clothes i smell
warm sun where you have been sitting
restless animals mew & brood
under the pillow in your boudoir

please you say please
            come in   why don't you
me a tall shadow tottering
                uncertain caller
& then in, in, i fall in where we do not
        breathe the air is so thick i
                yes you sway say yes undress
the garlic braid & then I very
                gently very
                    slowly I
    the two braids, brown
                please i say you say
            please
                    open the collar
                        hang the two
                    hot stings ,ear
                    rings, place the red lace
                        choker my elegant needle
                    point you wear your neck under
                            wide as a lake

        & then the six birds
    on your neck take turns
        talking in your throat

coffins:

take darkness in your hand
hammer shut loud noises
take that & you wince this
cramps my style you know
that the darkness with
which you hammer them
bang bang you slam open &
shut doors derelict with
silence shout silence hums
around us & within graves
we depend on power cords
we plug our hearts into
when someone goes off the
deep end & every thing the
wind the coats flapping the
sound of you & you are
                    at home
trying to hold on
nailing your ear down is
deafened every body
suddenly undefined
undefended deafened with
total darkness in

your hand & silence

on a slippery footing

step in the pool the red foot
print I write you with
spots over the tile

pulled like fruit
loops in your best towels
where I caught myself
suburban as they come

the leather foot I wear, sweating,
into immortality, immediate as sunburn
this is where the tribes of the dead flutter & flute
locusts make dry sticks in their throats

brides bachelors old men in agony young
maidens whose hearts mist
blood wet our faces
        like spring rain the slain men
                push with tremendous shouts
            thirsty with what they have
                    to say i must say

this is when I sacrifice myself
at the ditch the blood
leaps & glitters no it is
not black-clouded you are wrong

Godalming   Seward   Holmwood   Van Helming
        one by one they come but I do not
let them near hold my hand over the blood
until they know me tell me

where is Van Helming where Lucy where
Mina where will I lie this morning yet
I know too those I let near
will know and tell me what I need
to know at the dank trough

        the sirens
        wail so low so slow
        you can hear
        if you listen
        the shadows drink
        thick & sticky
        wet as nosebleed

        quick with electricity
        read the spells before them

    wish you would dip
    in my blood spilled at your feet
    this is my blood
        spilt for you
that you might write drink
that you might speak
                    my name

it's all in his head

for months & months

                  fly buzzes
cL-iNnk   **clinK**
                  klink clink
      clock in my head

       air is swervy
      i myself am
      a swallow
         i must swallow
my pride
       yes & my joy
   I can no longer wallow in

have heard it run
     the flies go round
& round   the shallow end
         of my head
hard-eyed cyclists in a velodrome

12

he resembles paraffin

                        only a woman pure
                        in heart can break
                        the spell only she can
                        hold him she must
                    give freely must unlock
                            must keep him
                              in her heart
                      beat keep time keep
                              him by her
                       side close as a coffin
                    close as key & padlock
                            he kneeling
                        the hit of hot wax

            the table of her forehead

                        till the cock crows
                          till light splashes
                                out of her
                            hand a lamp
                        post every lamp
                          a hot candle

            sounds coming off his throat
            a file drawn over soft wood

            this is what it boils down to
                    isn't it day after day
            snow falls out of our eyes
                time pockets the dream
                          carries it off
                on the end of a chain

sleeping sickness

have lain in twilight
lain in wait in want
since before I can remember
lover forever on hold
cool as a cobra

the small black room
the sense taken from me
am an undeveloped picture
bug mired on fly paper
negative light you let your gaze into

                              you don't know how
                              I have admired frogs
                    watched them pack in glucose
                         sandbag themselves close
                    though their veins fill with ice
                           they will not be crushed
                          they do not know but trust
                        the little machines that wake
                                         every spring

        what do i know of a body
        that though I ask lies
        stiff as rectitude refuses
        will not return a call
        release a single cell

am a bulletin pinned to the world's calendar
my bafflement a moth in an empty closet
something large and empty sticks
in my head my head stuck
shut like a broken telegraph switch

nothing happens I cannot speak
it is not eddies or scrawls or anything

so quick or certain it is a curtain yanked shut
    the closest I can think is a rusted spring

    why do you wonder that it falls
    that I shake in spasms
    frenzy to smell bodies
    moving when I taste you
    would bury my face in you
    feast on your soft flesh
    drink in the soft folds

            a monk released from confiscation
                breath dragged from a well

        hggnnghh hhnhhnn hggngghngh

            dead tree in winter my hands
        falling out of memory
        dripping on everything falling for
    ever from and never landing

he makes an important discovery

it openeth its mouth gapeth
wide as the gates as St.
Paul they sayeth
so that the very air playeth
over the soft skin
inside the mouth where the skin be-eth
thin and soft and heat goeth
with its every breath

to & fro in the night it moveth
down onto the warm dark waters
the river the male doth establish
it doeth this as is its nature
nothing but trouble from the word go

a place of its own being alone
it owneth a patch of watery darkness
tends it dogged as a tenant farmer
a strip of sand they pulleth
like a towel up on shore behind them
& keepeth it there on its mind
it lieth there & dreameth

night & day in sooth there
be-eth mud & sand warm
blood oozeth in their mouths

often it hath been attested the beast
doth bellow & quarreleth
beneath all knowing
other males shrug
lug their scales
through bedrooms

& when at last a lady lizard cometh
the roars the poor beast
doth let out of his hide go up
till his flanks shakketh
the very firmament
itself doth quaketh and water
sprayeth round his head
boulder or boat at the bottom
of Niagara Falls

whereupon he lasheth his great tail
and clapest his huge jaws in frenzy
the thunder he letteth go

& then it hath been seen
the poor stricken beast
his throat thrummeth like unto
the beating of Solomon's drums doth
clasp his beloved with his jaws withal
and verily, merrily like venison,
their very tails
entwine

oh listen Drac they're playing our song

Drac & Luce oh Drac & Luce
went down went down the dark
went down the dark together
it was knick & knack
they were neck & neck
were nick & nook on heather
both left wondering whether

they shld meet like this
shld meet in rainy weather
in feelings damp & peelings loose
damp as lambskin leather

cold winds & hail they weathered
in town & goosedown feathered
in snow & sleet they'd nethered
lay down in the all-togethered

well-dressed man about town

sky a torn membrane you can see
the signs read them for yourself
you know it is coming night
ploughed open the stars
thrown up like stones the horses
scream inside the fields
steam rolling eyes
wild lungings toppled houses,
carriages careen till the streets smell
turn to toffee and run in gummy streaks

that is why i never go out
without this rubber slicker
my loneliness crouches under
i become a darkgreen
lizard under shadow
when i wear it

throw it over my shoulder and take the night
with me i have to, it might not
be there when i arrive,

the night stretched so tight it fits
like memory i with effort swim inside
   night's blue transparency

        sky a mammary gland
            i suck on glad for it
        in my mouth every night
          wings slick & shiny
            as horseflies

blood brothers

yes I was there I always am
there when he tears
throats & the ditch fills

the creak of wings
crows coming to watch

                              we bend & sip the voices
              dampen our thoughts
we are glad after all
it is a time to talk

relieved to find our voices
have been hiding
all along beside us

  the blood in throats
whizzes past like ghosts

                  a wetting of lips
               a thickness in throats
             an incessant speaking
                  in tongues

it's not so bad

                                        the air
                    once you get used to it the air

you spend centuries rowing through air
    roaring your face & over
lean to this or that without feathers
learn to fuss without flapping
to do this after 230 years or so
                                        you say

you think it's easy, but it's not, you do it
                            even though it defies
        all logic all probability
my ability as an engineer my agility its wild
way past Leonardo & he knows it
I should be deified & he gets all the credit

you must know the night is not engineered
for this nor is my body for that
                        matter its nuts
& carriage bolts built for other things

                            take this jawfull of enamel
                        he quipped i am ill equipped

its no cinch getting this thing off the ground
getting it air borne believe me is quite the feat
you'll never get this off the ground they told me
old crate like that

                    when i put 5 quarters into the night machine
                            it gives me no ticket

21

this heavy-boned air craft forever
tilts forward threatens to nose-dive
drones its death-song into oceans & fields
Nazis such as yourself barrelling after
shouting your mouth off

nevertheless i know the way
                    thunder pops bones
                                        rivets snap
        off   /one by one
when you manage somehow to pull out
& you in your soft chair wonder
what's the big deal anybody could do it
        yawn with your blasé nights
        your jaded & herring
        boned days

                    you think I create a lot
of racket say i am for the birds
& what's more I can tell you you are dead
on they fall for me every single solitary time
I swoop or sweep past fleet swallow
when I flip up they weep & dream of sleeping
with me just at the last to land even
when I am a cormorant standing here
                        cellular phone in hand
finery spread to the breeze like a black flower
a flasher big shadows striding behind me
trying to dry the cellar from the residue of my flight

even then i am hunched
into this ridiculous pose
a terrible itch in my back feet
aching for some action even then
they stroke my plumage clinch me
in a flurry of shallows rummage
as if I were a trumpeter swan at night

      that's dumb
forget i say it's a cinch i am not
a warm membrane you can drain
      drum softly & play

      blood moving through me like a leaf

the city wakes

all night when i pry
day's lid off
i spy with my
little i
there it is
the small whine
something like a winch
a prayer when
it opens & then

a cry fits
into the box
neat as a spool of thread

the smell of night
moves moving the street
lamps at night hands upturned

light nests in
the cool drizzle of light
could be the movies
you are starring in
/staring at for that matter

all this leads me a
stray leaves me a
mazed into streets & tunnels
millions stream through
hiss in the vessels as they move
thousands of mussels in a pot

the whole city a bright oil
the noise & dazzle
cabs that scrape & clatter
forming wheels of light in the morning

he goes out walking after midnight

you'd never imagine
the lamp there
& then more
more & more

go by
shake off
light you feel
so smooth its skin
could be cosmetic
glamorous even

but it is
a dog that comes
out of water
& his skin
gives up
to shivers

only it burns when light falls
enormous candles you walk under
& they drip
sperm its white patches
congeal on the metal

it hits
& shatters
off your back

shudders till you feel
you are a shutter
whacking away in the light
that stutters past
your body blown
to ratshit

& still i am nervous

the narrow velvet
Lucy wears round her throat
no not what you say Van Helsing
not a bandage
it is a scarf actually
she is cold & she wears it
garter at its edges

two red filaments
demure as dream slip
past & under

all this pinned
at her throat
chaste as Mary herself
with a buckle

her lovely neck
fastened inside

the warm kiss
i put there
yes yes yes
quicken in her
when i slide it aside
when i slip
my love in her
gasps & spasms
Van Helm sings her hot
pinwheeled nights

        & after
the long languor of her
    waiting for relief
       in two tiny garnets
    rings i bring her
through the night's crevice
small service to her i love

she tries to save him

you got to lick this
you know that don't you
it's no good for you

    i mean look at what it's doin
    this thing is gettin bad
    real bad, believe me
    & I'm well you know a
        little concerned maybe
    you're hooked on it well
        you could be you know
    it's happened before first
        it's a sip here a sip there
    you come home a little tipsy
    shaking your fist at the salvation army

    oh I know it's just one
    with the guys & that's ok
    really it is I don't mind
    don't think I don't know how much
    you look forward to that

i know it's once in a blue moon
        only then it's one
    for the road & in no
time at all there you are rolling
in bleary-eyed & puffy at dawn
        & that's it you gone
about as far as you can go
thank your lucky stars you missed
    the breathalyzer

& me all night worryin & worryin has somethin happened
well it might it might Drac you know yourself
that new family 's moved in next door all crosses
& curses I'm scared Drac real scared & I wish you would
think of me once in awhile me & the kids
we're scared sick every night sittin up waitin & watchin
and the landlord she's itchin' to repossess the place

                    it's a filthy habit to tell
              the truth it's filthy & disgustin
                          is what it is

                              hey c'mon
                    you gotta admit it Drac
                      things have gotten a
                         little out of hand
                      you know it don't you

              face it my man
          yr finally an addict
          & you gotta get help
        right away

all the faces

thousands of faces spread
the night streets a shower
torn kleenex remnants from
a wedding that's been
suddenly cancelled

      they spread & soften
       float upon the dark
             currents your eyes
      bright with pollen

                     evasive as starlings when i appear
                     your print dresses blow
                     easy on the breeze i emit
                     the startling way they press
                     against your breasts
                     your nipples
                     hard in the cool air

      & then morning
peels night off the skin
ript back the way they used
to do women's faces to make them new

only nothing grows back
there is no beauty here
nothing covers the carmine agony

      i take back lie
     my eyes wide open
all night long a flayed animal
afraid of the flowers that flit
past their sharp petals
clicking at the window like heat
that clacks the day into broken light

our lives our houses

the bodies you eat &
    sleep in the wall
papered compartments you sit
separate rooms you live in
unhappy guests comport yourself
            with strained courtesy

most of them are shaded in
varied as maps of the empire
splotches of pink or it is night
& a furnace rumbles in your chest
the water meter wheels on & on
toilets flush cupboards bang shut

beds   tables   chairs   desks
—bones you anchor your flesh to
        all the connective tissue
you tear when you move and fall
in love focussed as a flash
    light between them
trying to tack your life together
                    with strips of light

        the want your flesh carries in its wake
        & is lost when you are gone
                        the bones talk gravely
        visit in the cavities houses hold

during the day the tables & chairs
scrape across sunlight
sharp as paring knives in butter

            by night the startled beds
            now and then rattle

maybe it is

there is a flying
we cannot avoid a flying
machine in you too its two
wings flutter your pink chests
get tired waiting
it wants to fly
it wants to get out
you wonder if
you can afford this

maybe it is an angel
maybe it is not
so black & creaky

it is in your throat
it creaks & craws
so low you do not notice
when you do it
bleeps & whistles past
the crooked turns
your attention takes
slams past your hearing

except at night
when you turn
on the switches & tweeters
plug in the green gas lights
you can hear it twitter
you know it croaks
the trapped & wet thing
that is your mouth
flaps in a revving sound
you wonder if it is
something reviving

night & day
there is a flying
in you &
what is really
something—

& bold strokes
of thunder

hygiene lesson

did you brush yr teeth
she sd you better

brush after every meal
if you know what's good
for you that's what
they say

pretty good set a snappers
you got there mister but
you don' watch it yr gonna
stain yore dentures is what

boy oh boy you know
you really better
brush yr teeth
dint yr mom learn you nothin'

's a fine set all right but
you don't look after 'em
you're gonna lose 'em
sure as im stan'in here
you are quite a mess
is what you are mister

& another thing
i don' min' sayin'
it'd be a fine sight better
know wha' i mean
yuh better give 'em what for
yuh wanna click

know what you got you got
a social problem is what
breath like that
you just better
smarten up & start lookin'
after yrself a little bit better

red men ace

yeah well what you expect
him & cooley they're in cahoots

i mean open yr eyes fer chrissake
bloody reds course they stick together

they want ya tuh believe
they are harmless they got bad press
Dracula he's just a poor
misunderstood little boy

don't you believe it
they're bloody well dangerous
contagious is what

they know damn well what they're up to
you ask me, wanna stuff their faces
& don't lift a finger to earn it
want a piece of yr pro
perty is what
in perpetuity
can't wait to lay
a hand on it

got to hand it to them on a platter
it's pubic enterprise and nothing but

want it so bad they can taste it
them & them bleedin'
heart liberals

world without end

i mean no harm
where i brush you
burn like smoke till it hurts
my eyes the rush i feel
i am agent of largesse yes
ardent for a world without

end the universe is a giant
we are inside & we bump
the walls in big clumps
the pain when we hit

it is against that
i work inject my serum
it is i who pierce the membrane
the sternum which keeps us apart

it is my spirit dissolves the clots
my spit keeps the sticks & stones
streaming with blood the whole galaxy
haemophilic with love
breaks the lumps of antigen that get in the way

we can crush them with our breath
my love

he plays his part

ladies i am only
what you have come
among the leaden skies
thick from your laden & ladled lives
to expect the hot piercings

eyes dark looks so inscrutable
i might have stepped un
scrupulous as the black prince him
self out from the purple romances
you engorge yourselves on
slamming them down like doughnuts

day after day you sit in your peig
noir housecoat slacks & toast & sweatshirts
dressed as usual in late-afternoon boredom
tucking away every last crumb

you grow obese ladies
on capes & tux the strength
with which I pull myself
up & down the slippery walls
you dream your want in
say you cannot wait
sigh damply into
your tattered books

you are ready for elaborate gallantry
hints of desire so uncontrollable
you shiver at the window fear
ever after one night I might
actually pop up in scrape & cape
from which there is no escape

            look I hate to admit it but
I get a little tired of this the faintings
moonpale swoonings whenever I reach the sill
            the limp bodies no more
responsive than playdough
me faking the class act
fading into middle age
& growing a middle

                              to tell the truth
                              sometimes i feel
                              im nothing more
                              than an over
                              grown mosquito
                              faint fever
                              you get off on

fox & geese

what about this then
it's fox & chicken
that's what it is
you & me playing "pie"
& that's a fact

there you are scrawny
neck blowing on yr hands
wrinkly as wind your neck
that is you are
a pullet squawky with eggs
you haven't let go
you've got to admit
you're quite the sight

you stand there blinking
& there i am that's me
over on the other side

hi i say i can see you
from here across the white
paths we stamp cold from

I run across the henhouse criss
crossing its coarse smells
the ones you roost upon crisis after crisis
around & around the pie on aching hopes
I chase my arctic breath I wait
my chances I know my chances
are good where you brood darkness
I know this is archaic
anarchic enough even for you

out of the blind white land
             look I say we got to stop
this running around I am running
out of breath people are starting to talk
this is no good for either of us
    we will grow arthritic

            let's face it
        you and your matrimonial dreams
                    they're no more than amonial schemes

                                i got under yr skin
                                    & you got me
                            where you want me

            you got hold of me
        & won't let go

    just hold on tight
        & don't let go

                my feet are a killin' me
            just hold on tight & don't let go

wild goose chase

but I don't care

> **haha-**
> **haha ha-aa HAW**

I'm only pretending

> I can't wait till it happens
> me I'm fed up with this

wild goose chase believe me
I would rather see a show of taste
a little colour at your neck
I'd ruffle in wind, real romantic
                & delicate as if for
once I caught you   napping
       aromatic with sleep

& you you gone & lost yore head
aincha huh you gone & went mental on me
now yuh'll be a bone flapping in wind
         splashing in wine

ill hang around avid for you
utterly dedicated pie-eyed with disaster
knowin you are lookin for a part in Ovid

> well forget it this is Canada
> we don't do them things

> but don' worry eh
> that's me all right
> a flutter in your heart
> red flame at your throat

evil ocean

pterodactyls pull time apart
sometimes in long tearing sounds
sometimes they pull it up
like carpet glued to the floor of the universe
till it is wet & sticky viscera
they get stuck in   \claws or no clause

crack their knuckles
fidget & pretend theyre tough
they like to strut around
in tight leather flight jackets

        the pterodactyl where it sits
            in a hill is wondering
       when will it let gravity out
          worries will its body hiss
       embarrassingly like a tire
            when it happens
         will it go flat its valve
     having given up the ghost

                    its last gasp
               & frost closes in
          popping digits & shaking
         chains bright as eternity

                     will it lose
             its nerve will it be
          brought to a standstill

they rev their cardiovascular systems
gangs of pterodactyls their fingers
stretched from all that pulling
on millennia pulling on gloves
aeons of time tugging on them

& so they make slick suicidal death
defying swoops down the back
roads backbones sky spirals with & then
rumble tumble stumble
        back to weight
picking rodents from their teeth
           like peking ducks

      all ducts on go its flight
      plans filed somewhere in the front panel

                    its little helicopter
                    brain the ptero
                    dactyl chops
                  up the sky dreams
               pain hopes for panic
      warm blood one of them imagines
            it will be a holy terror
         thinks if only it can think
        things through it will last
    a long long time

I'm all ears

this is strictly bad
news I'll try to break it
to you gently I think
as a gentleman it is
only fair to tell you after all
this time
year in & year

out I'm still hanging
around look you have only
to look over there
see that
pack of wild dogs look

at the ears

see them ears

that's me there I'm all ears
've fallen terribly in arrears
& what is more I am
all yours go ahead
you know what you want

scratch me behind whiskers
rub me on whispers
in the ear I will perk
to your call rise
to your friendly touch

they find their tongues

it is in the soft parts the throat finds
new shapes it is in these moments it happens
it is there it starts
        at first clumsy
and slow and then after eons
light , quicker more fluent

toads stick their tongues out
                              learn to spell
              death
in clicks & buzzes

in the airshaft flesh bulges and folds
it is there blood starts up air
floods tunnels and then blood

                starts to talk & I
                  stop & stoop
I listen, drink down warm words
                    , their milky effluence
they glisten for conversation
till I am drunk, stupefied with message

        your heart releases
     a flight of words
every month you hatch blood
goes swish goes wishes
wishes all this to your head
going out of your head, affluent with it
shows when your chest winnows
sounds past your ear

fluttery as gills I put my ear
                    my lips to your lips
        inside the slippery air

    the muscles under you breathe
    the cartilage opens
    two lips press together
    oh two lips in heaven

no matter what they say you say we are
                involved in one another
        what you say to me up past
the windy ridge your collar bone makes
the small river it takes past
                                the black reeds
the sighs and separations

know it is for you Lucy
3 million years in your bones

why do you think
i throw myself off cliffs of air
spend eons learning to roll & soar
tow capes of thunder behind

THUNDER THUNDER THUNDER

go ahead im all years
all yours all ears the eras
roaring ahead behind around me your waiting
rumbling by unheard go ahead
ask me, ask me anything

well yeah at first it was kind of funny
at first it was hard i heard
the terrible pull in the chest & shoulders
it sounded a bit like ropes & pulleys
the crisis of turning the corner
so I didn't crash at every pain
not knowing
when it would end

my mom scolded me don't you go
& bash your face on the wind you want that
you seen hockey
players haven't you
you seen them, you want that

i was quite the sight at first
i'm little more than a loose id, right
the whole thing 's one big swamp
it looks like I'm stuck in

& then it's the insects i'm adolescent &
it's insects the sky is suddenly jammed
with them they think well it's their time
their number's called & they're hittin the airwaves
till it's WW II they've got a bead on you
they're a long way off but they got me
on radar i can't foil them & then
                    they're there let me tell you
                    about the insects—the first few

centuries i would arrive face splattered
                    with them & all
            those i hoped to call on

it's about time you got here they say
time, hell, i say, i lost my bearings

    it's about time I've come I say
how would you like to make time

        you could stay the night
                with me

to & fro I grow lucid

oh yeah, the early days I flew
by the seat of my pants
after a few eras I got the knack of it
I grew lucid, the balance came

back in my ears they stopt
buzzing, almost, & my hands
after awhile weren't so chapped anymore
    the feeling began to come back
    it even got so's I got the speed
right & didn't sear the eye
brows & moustache too bad

      night flying, night flying was the worst
            nothin' worse
          but I had no choice right
                  way I learned
                  a few tricks

          even learned to throw my voice
            sky she's one big tent &
        KKHHKH   KKHHKK you know
   the tongue on top of the mouth

   KHHK you just let er go

you follow your voice around
like Mulroney he loves his voice
follows it everywhere tho no one else will

  I mean this was past the first edition
  it was way past it had become an addiction, practically
  & yet there was a beauty in it, a grace
            a certain ease

got so's I could spiral night like a barn
swallow nigh onto morning I would cork
                    screw move
                              on the air
                                        with such $\mathcal{E}$'s

            up & up & up & then

        down,
drawn down into that black

                        bottle & gulp
            till i think my god i will drown

                god i was beautiful
                                        am\
        beautiful loop after loop after loop

                O's &
                        $\mathcal{A}$'s (ahhhs)   this is awe

            some &
    loose E's
                (Lucy's in the sky you know)

exquisite as a kite

sky-writer i wrote the world wrote to
        the world too asking love
and it loved back, those days
the elegant curls and bends
our cheeks let loose, sighing

          oh yeah she was all there
              the DNA spinning
         the bones Lucy gave all
        of you i so much want
            to be welcome in

      all this all night long
cinnamon moon hot sulphur blood-red
     the way I leak out over its face
         till it much resembles Io and
then there's the 700 mph winds
think how they gouge the face of Neptune
till you must suppose I am Lucifer himself

            till it will never end I think
               there it is, a lot
                like a, a tea
          biscuit is what & why
        don't you invite me
      in Lucy remove the tea
     cozy & pour all the fragrance

           it's all so crazy
        we can count count
          count your bones
      you say no sweat sweet lady
    i drum on the skull the sky forms

grins i swoop under
it's ok i got a few
tricks up my sleeve

i am gorgeous my god i am
so beautiful when i

throw myself onto night
throw myself around its neck
exquisite as a kite

sweet Lucifer I am stuck on this
my sleek hot motor
the sweet smell of oil
wind whistling over
everything in my dreams
tumbling brightly the bird
in fear trumpets

even when things go wrong
it's not bad, really
when i crash & burn
when i fall into the drink

you are a lake
hot rocks sink
and sizzle in

they paint water

                   birds at night brooding bluesy
                her neck a clarinet, mugged
             the warm estuary find our
          selves at it breeding, reeds & all

the red stains on the rocks
where you blow paint from your mouth
and fish and birds happen

sounds of limestone smooth
rain the pelicans scraping
stars off the rain every morning
the bright birds take to

                        the air all day
                                screaming

                        sounds falling out
                              like frogs

he has seen the night

I have seen the light & it burns
holes in my head the sky hot
holes in my hands
candles overflow with time
the blue flame enters
the empty cathedral

have seen the signs have seen
night & the coming of night
my people and I would swing
past them past the last
posts step through the acid spray
the stench of ashes & piss

and yet when
we laugh
my lady & i
small flo
wers po
p thro
ugh the s

now min
i at ure umbre
llas, lit
tle dro
ps of bloo
d spot the she
ets

we go down
into darkness hand in hand
hand & hand together
the dim lantern smoking
the jervy music
earth a long quiet fizz
a sewing machine, running

we who have come across
the cold calling
my lady it is me
it is only me Mina
my love a love only
Pluto could remember
you told me so yourself

me my lady carrying your
garden of flesh
down into the damp
thick wet lily

it smells a little
like beg
onia

awakenings

came back from somewhere
i never knew
dazed with moving
dizzy with jerks
syllables popped underfoot

ssS-s
ttuh t*uh*
uh uh

uh,, ter
rrr u!h h'

u-h
uhhh

u;h **UH**

found a place i knew
remembered dimly

& there was you
& there was music
the smell of water was in
whose loveliness i entered
you said
i moved inside music
the rust in my knuckles dissolving
voices inside unjamming
a door long stuck,
noise from the colours, starting

there was the smell when it rained
& poems after you read streets opening
something small only large too
something inside getting larger
breathed clouds red grass grew in
                    and birds, talking

          sounds that moved over like june rain
          smells wet as water colours
                                        & running
                    warm & clean
              & then cool

              there were doors opening
                            & yellow laughter
                  splashing into the streets
              & air on our faces like love, rushing

entered rain like june you said brushing
the smell when you read the water the air large
moved over us in a poem that was yellow rain
voices fluent as doors on the river breathed birds
            rain behind our eyes falling

          our faces in a place
        falling out
  colours go

          ing ng ng a
                      wayyyy
            & i

we ntb ack so
         mew her ei ca
nt re re rem
      ember her
              e ex-
      cept iw as

                  t here
       the rew asmus   ic
           an dt he rew as you ,

yo us aid
    th e r e   wa s
                   you

she waits

feel my body
                    get hot & hotter &
tremours wave after wave & still
                    i am in rapture

                         it sidles toward me
                         long slow muscle
                    smooth as brown wind smooth
                         water that does not sink

                         plasma in the shade
                         the muscle follows
                    , follows, flows into itself blows
                    into its own tongue flip flip flip

                         wet as the grass
                         blunt as want itself

                    muscle trails itself into blood
                              slides into itself
                    molten bottle, foot into shoe
                              , moving

          watch where it parts
     the grass I can see coming
     could be a comb you blow on
     could be some strangeness
        our bodies align on

it is on a mission
slides over stones & valleys
my body forms the alleys
you smell cucumbers, sliced

in the grass & shrubs dumb
slack-kneed with something
I have not felt only know
it comes I know not where

it's in the blood

purple fever in you dream people
can't help it if I pull on
my face for the night & here I am
ready as a condom as flexible

if that's not stretching a point
it could be a highway
robbery reams & reams of me
enough to be her
O her etic
etc. in this real M
this wild expedition

the goitered wind its aspirations its it
erations hope you too will
be smitten will come
down with poetry will be yourself
bitten by sounds in your limbs
loud as a twin
otter more X
-tatic than blood
poisoning you a swollen membrane
a sore throat

the world gives up its static the condition
spreads the red con
tagion the plague unlatches
strange off-key songs
all night long

he goes calling

upon my word
the Wardian case I carry
my wayward heart is growing in
a manner which can only astonish

myself you have
my word on it the freshest
hue the sweetest
fragrance no orchid could release
I have brought from far away
intend to plant it lady in your glass
house put it in the cutglass vase
sunlight warms now to blue & yellow
its soft bruise, your bare shoulder
the bare curtain blowing
a chemise in early light

this is me & this is the gardener
in mid swipe I whisk by , humming

past the glasshouse its stems fizzing
sago cocoa Jesuit's bark ipecacuanha
cassia capivi past the two-wheeled machine
shaving green off the yard like soap, clacking
whisker whisker whisker the silver blades say
this is : :
Budding's Grass Shearing Machine

the statuary is polite pretends not to stare
when you nod to the gnomes looking down
as if there were treasures under their feet
as if the parasols did not soak up pastels nearby
as if the air did not feel smooth as taffeta
as if the place were not soaked with pumps & syringes

underfoot the wet squish of manure
the frantic twizzled paths
look like pipe cleaners kids have bent
rockery glued onto the blue
          eye the pond opens
sleep in its eye the vast
cast iron vase a dog
drowned in, his bark too
from the kennels loping past
the poultry house astringent with ammonia
swings flower beds stuffed as pillows
and insects squirming everywhere
there will be a movie of this some time

the hasp they open to morning
pansies jostling creamy puffs wasps
saw the breeze the lazy rasp
berries) a lady in the garden weeding
steelblue fork in her hand

all the shapes the sharpness falling off
the palisades blurring into blue-green the sun
glows past a fountain full of snakes
there is a miracle a mirage
the way water twizzles under air
the tweezered breeze
                    tick tick I will say, walking
                         tick tick my feet say

                    inside know what is waiting
         behind the frames greener than melons
          the curtains smell from smoke & gravy
                     the walnut hall in antlers
                    hung from coloured glass
               the clear blues the deep orange
             the astonished eyes of taxidermy
                  stag faces hares ears boars
                  tusks a horse head replete
     in reins & veins holds steady monkeys
                         sit still & listen
                   the whickers & whinnies
                  the whole ménage a whimsy
                  cats foxes rams the entire
                     head of a carriage dog
                        hooks in its jaw
             : panoply of a broken ark   & then

                   the parlour moist bulb you grow in
                      sealing-wax reds you rise from
                        a pre-Raphaelite painting
                 stir from a gilded urn a writing table
              sherry carafe the fluted body, cut neck
                      carmine choker at your neck
                    your voice forms a thin green
                    film on the glass we float & will
                         mix like gases in
                  the bluegreen swish of your dress
           feel of its velvet your hair long and warm
          this is what I find
                         blushing in your skirt brushing
                      the gold & blue wallpaper
     how pleased with my pink present
                              my word
               your astonished eyes will say
     it is you you will say it is you

periodically

every month
the moon cracks
never fail at full moon
it cannot nor can I
renege
i break out
beak & all

dark clouds renegade moon
pops out
,swollen

every month
Canis Major Ursa Major
it falls out of the dipper out of the canister
and breaks

blood red moon
sudden at your lips
i kneel
quick as a ruby
throated humming bird
at nectar
kiss in absolution

the harvest moon

stars
in the sky
our eyes
break through
in blisters

echolalia

                    the first thing you should know
                    about me is   i am
                    a sound poet
                                i wind up &
                    throw my voice
            into the tent
        : like that

? how you like that
            neat don't you think
    all the loops in the system

    some smart guy said well
what's the point
        it's canvas isn't it
        & you say yeah well so what
        it's paint yr smearing there
        all over the canvas yr words are paint

he's a real pain in the ass that guy

                    the important thing is
                        i take soundings see
                    i try to hear myself
                            try to hear you hearing
                    yur eyes grow green & big
                        that's how i find myself that's how
                            i find you
                        i can hear where you sizzle
                    & pop

we meet in gardens

am a gardener
you know this
guardian of scent
gorgon of yes
yes i was /
scent to you
sent for
you send me
to tend
tend to send me

things you tend to
say you have always
known know now
your cool evening
strolls where white
faces bob the stems
bloom & blow

the crunch of gravel the sound of
dogs across night
your painted faces
blurred & pastel
quick smears on night

you have escaped glass
your pressed faces looked out from
you have felt them felt it
indecent because it draws you practically in
candescent the fact it draws
you smell shining everywhere
faint fogging and even
tumours on the mirror
break out
in scarlet fever winter measles kids from school

it is then i come out of night
the evening opens & i brush past
you waiting in your evening
gown have grown into this
unease you know i am
a rumour somewhere beside your room
inside you where curtains move like lungs

smell a scratch under your listening
you from your easel lithe with mauve
could be a weasel could be
breath weighted on sulphur

something thick a match you think
thick thick as a match spurts
all the life i gather in my arms
warm where your dresses stammer
my yearning stalks you grow
come to sing your iridescence all moon upon

Pennanggalin

a mouth dangling
entrails
hangs like loose hair
she fills herself in blood
angling down her thorax
till her intestines shine & stretch
her smile slithers behind her like slang
sloppy with wanting

people tack thorns around windows
so she will snag & poke holes in her humour
tangle helplessly there hopelessly in love
taken with door frames and door jambs
they hope she would get hooked on latches &
footnotes

Pannanggalan soaks her entrails in vinegar
drinks vinegar till she shrinks
sloops back in her body waiting
a bottle waiting for her return
lost genie back from a binge

do not let her drip on you
do not let her grin at you
do not let her kiss you
above all do not let her
get a grip on you

if she does you will break
out in sores everyone can see
where the blood has fallen
do not walk under
trees she roosts there entrails dangling

spirits herself away on hash
hushes there she suspends her spit
she is a bag of trash & she scratches & scratches
it's slash & burn in this undergrowth
Pennan there without a stitch
                 quick slash
         pulls her entrails through her teeth
                     grooms herself
            till she is neat
                    , like thread

he waits at the gate

why do i feel as if
i were a flame then, a blue flame
a lit candle whey-faced i bring to you
your face a frame for what in you i would see

why do i flicker when you bend
to me why do i lick at your dark
shores your gentleness everything
bends, everything blends

but i do fear you
will pinch me
out between your in
difference & i think i
will rock be
wildered at the iron grate

sky over us, spilt milk
the morning spoilt & sour

why do i hope then
you will lift me in your hand
let my life spill
your face bright with flour

your skin full
luminous with lampsmell

i want the world
fallen away
from our shoulders my love
& after, drops of wax
& a cat, calling,

why don't you breathe in
my mouth why
don't you make me
yours why don't you
take me in from the street

      it could be a warm reef
      we pulled a sheet over
      all the darkness in us
      our mouths full of stars

twisting the light away

you always wanted it
always dreamt yourself
imagined that you would

twist the key at the side of my heart
unlatch it one quiet evening
let yourself in when I wasn't there
you would twist your self side
ways so light would not come off
you would slide off it glide by invisible
stirring up dust as you went

i knew you would be
there have heard you
yawn the sheets
wrapped round

what makes you
so sure of yourself
what makes you

think I would climb in
with you turn
out the light
pull the lid shut
as I did

always knew you
would be there waiting
lost file
on the other side
of the cabinet
the far side of the room

there is no other

knows they live for this
climb from stone rooms
to carry down comatose lives
on their shoulders the blandness of husbands
the housebound stories they have heard

want to call dreams down from their sleep
needing no explanation nor wanting any
call from their dreams &
there are streets
full of taxis
throbbing

the lovers climb
into and out of
their soft pulse
touch all night long
the sweet lubricity
the beautiful ache that tells them
you are alive
you need no other
there is can be
no other
expiation

night freight

scratched our eyes with longing
the long dream the somewhere scream
a freight train leaping

                                        country & then
                                        my shoulder, heavy, up
the hills follow the raw wounds up // around
                                        a stomach hacked open
                                            a bright eye staring
you sitting, see, the cars, frightened
writhing behind the train's body
            under the moon crushed
the bright track, infections of light

                        *

            sky lined with snot & ashes
            the sharp smell you can hardly
            breathe when the train squirms
            & hisses in the tunnel

                            the sky turns to
                    slag you float on , sharp ache
                        migrates across your back

                fresh as a fly as fleshly
                down into the creosote
                we sweet sinners go
                giddy in defiance

        & the laugh you will laugh
will be stepping suddenly into no wind
your neck its long perfume

                              imagine we will go
            among clinkers
                  our eyes will go
on and off, gas lamps, candles
                                    , day running over
            the heart's inflections
the long whistle that hurts our ears
the darkness and the morning
turning up its handlebars
      like a moustache

moving dirt

                              moving dirt
                        it's a matter of that
                         a case of caring
                              for earth
                         i cart north
                         every spring

lairs they call them the liars
they have grown glutinous with spite
these are sites of letting go
here you can order only nightmare
you know this well this is
consummation you must want & fear

          you are indebted to me it's a matter of distribution
                    actually i spread myself thin i spread
                              dirt all over London
                         the house by the asylum
                    another in Piccadilly, Whitechapel

               the others gather
               & seek some way
               they might pull it all
               together some spoor the clues
               night runs to

               meanwhile i busy myself
          occupy the ditches in their reports
                    forever hauling dirt
               a pack-rat gone awry you think
night & day i disperse disseminate
sidestep their glue & nails
put off the start where it all ends

all the machinery that consolidates
undermines your very id
eology your fear i shld do this
champion of distribution, deferral

        all the well-bred Brits
        their tight-lipped tightwad economy
        suppose they should keep control
        fear i will devalue their
                tight currency of blood

they call imperiously for turnkeys & tourniquets

would put an end to my largesse
my sweet liquid expenditure

red tide i hammer in their vaults
flood the most precious holdings

a dismal scientist speaks

it's all there
they see red see him
red menace anarchist of change
priest of plenitude
burglar of bodies & blood
above all the inflation he introduces

above all they want to stop
the excess of expenditure
turned to no gain
the scandal of that

they would keep everything
to themselves the secret
safety boxes they seal and lock
look more devout than if they were chaste
wore chastity itself
thank god they have
money themselves they say

believe they must fortify replenish
there can never be enough
they do not have enough
must resist this emission of energy
this pick-pocket of lips & purses

i say the bloke must have sold his soul
some god of transoms & thresholds has
him in his hip pocket

someone must set off in hot pursuit
someone must stop the haemorrhaging
there are leaks in the system

the bourgeois of blood know
the reds are at their aging
throats breaking & entering the old
codes the double book-keeping entries

    say their currency must be kept
       out of circulation
       out of the wrong
         hands

haberdasher

why this secresy
why does Van Helsing
glove himself in hints by day
          fasten guesses round his waist
          why does he dress himself
     every day in supposed stories
tie them carefully under his chin

          what about the suppressed stories
                    stored in his clinic there
          among the suppositories & old adages

why all story long
     am I allowed
          no name

                    lord god almighty they got Lord
                    Godalming on their side
                         i kid you not
                    they got all the names
                              the bastards

who does he think
he is who is he anyway
to take off in the plot
each night as if he were
a night pilot in a harbour

                              untie it & plop
out it goes   /all over the couch
          he sleeps on future
tense lives off delays

tease of never that's him all right
positively enjoys the way they hurt
the goddamn harbinger why does he
never take a bender go on a binge

why does he so prolong
the end who
does he think
i am
any way

the dog & the moon

blink one week &
the light becomes
a dab of mercury

corner to corner you blink
cornea to cornea the light passes
a yellow membrane opens & closes
    over & over
eternal shutter in the sky

        a marble into morning rolls
month after month you watch

    dog bundle her darkness
drag it near the sun
all our bones she's dug & cured
dutiful as a dry-goods clerk
she lies down inside her ribs
& the band plays bone marrow

      tomorrow there'll be
a rabbit in her heart
bits of me in her jaws
bandy-legged with regret
grateful for attention

solecisms at the door

well let's get serious
  there's nothing my
          sterious

            what do you think
            it's a snap being a bat
            man you better think
            again about steroids it's a crying

                shame the way they treat you
                you think it's glamorous it's all
                in your hands all auto
                graphs and photo opportunities
                you think everywhere you turn

                        it's romance here intrigue there
                            here a trigue there a mance

                    it's a trigue with a mance
                    ive been learning to do

        truth is it's
      a walz through men
        ace of love ram
    bunctious for lunches
  perrier & grapefruit with my beau
      tiful people pitiful
    & bloody marys for chasers

                what it really is is you get caught
                    in rain you get hooked
                no not on some torrid affair
                though you do get hung up
                    in the black wet boughs
                    you get hooked on rain
                wait for it to wash your face

                                  clean as marble
                       but all you get is shrivel

                                    your skin
                     isn't sanforized the cape is not
                     preshrunk nor is it sanitized
                     what do you expect it's 1895

                  Bram's done all he can do he's got the latest
                     gadgets in here brought in typewriters
                  we're completely up-to-date in this novel

        got to give him good marks for enterprise
        hell he's even got recorders
        he's got it taped man & i bet
        you didn't even know he had them

        technology's closing in fast
        not much time for us marvels
        you know we're about to croak

                  you better do up your rubbers eh
                     you better snap out of it quick

                             like I was saying the cape it's not
                                   the cat's meow you take
                             one look and you think luck eh
                          you think the lucky son of a bitch
                          gets to zoom around like superman
                                  you think it's good luck
                 it's a charm
                                    I'm a hunchback or something
                          you think I'm a special umbrella right
                              some kind of fancy hombre

86

terrible gaucheries

that's about the size of it
your petty & pathetic fantasies

the real truth is I simply
capsize I come undone one cap
size later I come completely un
buttoned unzipped unsnapped
I'm finished kaput finis brought down
to size pretty soon its

squish

SQUISH

sQuISShhh

sqUIIsH

nothing
to write home about nothing
but ish nothin' but shiver unshriven & shrivelled
you're washed out completely washed up
yr down the drain & no pension
not a thing to fall back on

sure you try and fuel up on darkness
try to suck it up but in these conditions
you snorkel more than anything
its air yr snorting

soon you are chattering yes lady c.
chatting her up as best you can you shrunk
little beast wet as a weasel every fantasy
your thoughts of touching her softness
shrink wrapped & ript to shreds
you haven't a shred of decency left
rag flapping in wind, one of cooley's
                    interminable crows

                    me at the rain at your door

night Ambassador

you look puzzled , pause
why is this happening
to you
there should be well
appointed men in navy
blazers true
& their eyes their eyes
should be dark blue
& burning

blue a bag pulled from the night lake
heavy from swimming & cold
i am slow
i am old
as wells

the buzzes in slow motion the e
motion the crack in my back
i come out of

you & your blood loud
as a windmill sway
you say why should i
be an embezzler
when i nuzzle

wonder why i guzzle your light
you wonder out loud
how it happens
so fast how it spreads
by word of mouth

i come out
the crack in your neck you let
in the wind the dark
a whisper in your face & smelling
the bog i step from steeped in
the shadows i do not cast

ladies and gentlemen

buzz from the men
what is happening what
is being done here

he can appear when he wants
when he wills, and where,
out of thin air he can
appear   & vanish
                louder buzz, consternation
    pull back they pull back)
in all things can he appear

fogs thunder rats owls
foxes dogs crows frogs
wolves   ]growing alarm
bats cats hats pulled
inside out the cracks
in casement window sills
even in the still & camphored air

]shouts of anger, fear
i say to you vapour viper
scruffle scrofula the scruff of your necks
        ]fear, anger, shouts
    they crowd in, they strain
yes in the very rain that varnishes
these gates we stand beside
    leaves its dark stain
he's there he's here I'm afraid
when he pulls his vanishing act
    [mumblings they are anxious
        what is to be done

what are we doing here
you are probably wondering
it is our task to keep him
horizontal as if he were
in a hospital bed where he is powerless
for once he is in an upright position
he is   [apprehension, what is this
powerless]ahhhh for once he is
in an upright position]what
whatwhatwhatwhatwhatwhat
he is virtually irresistible
almost impossible to keep out
noise nearly drowns the speaker
he shouts is shouting now

out in the cold out of your
women's minds

you must not think

am on the third side of darkness
you must not think
                    it is not
        lonely here
                    i hear
your blood thud

        my ears
rustle because it is restless
being near myself as if i held the sea
to my head held my head
to the sea in its shell
roars far away as forever

        shall we not then
        meet where the window sky opens

                        luminous moon
                    the oceans rising
                        i wash
                        up on shore

        salt spray in your face
            red spray
to the tips of your hairs
the sky dizzy & thankful
            with stars

in name only

all the ways to move me
out of your lives
anoint me as if i were hives
you poured ointments on

vampire succubus judas geek
vlad the impaler & arent you glad
paler than you think supple
enough to slip through
soft shoe on my slippers past
the names you would tip over
press me under squash me with
the books you have bound
yourselves to would put me in
some known character Nosferatu
for starters nefarious man Wurdaluk &
not a word of a lie Man That Was the
Undead the Thing there are others this is
not counting Stregoica witch ordog pokol
a big bristly array against me your diaries
the journals Mina Harker reads & collates

feel in these names this coffin
as if i am a sardine in a tin
german asparagus kept from the light
you have canned me in your sardonic novels

i'm warning you you can't count me out
you should know I am Count Dracula

you are so sure you have
got me where you want me
but you should know i will slip past
silent as U-boats
slippery as sleep itself
could if i wished sink your ribboned sentiments

even as you write now
you think you can write me off
write over me if you look
close you can see
beneath your thick-stockinged letters
if you were to shade them in
you would see suddenly a
water mark
i flow in
& out of

conjugal delight

within the tissues of night
at night Lucy gasping

when i enter her
chamber the spasms
the hot breathing
our utter suffusion

what we give to one another what issues
we are led to have bled for this
consummation these
tiny pin
pricks where
desire thickens
the air turns vermillion

Helsing from Amsterdam will never no
nor Holmwood nor Hollywood nor Seward
understand
how bodies join & conjoin
our circuit of desire
how conjugal it is

the jugs our bodies are
the movement through bottles
the jugular warms the neck
red wriggles
from body to head

an economy of blood
through our skins trace
the stars conjunctions
their clear ice
we know no compunction
our bodies, hot engines, race & embrace

the bright blood
the heart's action

       we drink & are whole
      periods of the moon
    moan where air
     passes over
            the bottle

it's a different story

it's your story isn't it
you would teach me

you flirt with loss
hint you may lose

me may lose your mind one day
that's it isn't it your nar
rative near and new
ly broken nearly ruined so
me one's taken a wrecking
ball to it til it's dust & rubble
twisted supports & someone
's going to pay for this
through the nose if you have your way
cunning in your account

you cough & rub
can't believe your eyes
what is happening

to you I am a character beyond
the grave beyond your jurisdiction let loose
a noise beyond reach a silence past reproach
something wrapped in a chamber
through whose walls the winds pass like silver

your twisted thoughts think of that
hi that's me inkpot in the other room
the door your story will open on
rusted pins & oh
pinions is what you see

I who have lain in a dry zucchini skin
   am now a raw fact
scale the superstructure
welding torch in hand oh lady
         I carry a touch for you
know we both will be brought to a bright star
an altar in whose fonts you dip
fearing affront the touch that sears

             a bowl of fire you
             will become a hot
             flame in your throat
             your mouth a smoking trough
             where we weld ourselves together
             wed our desires to steel
             no one can touch

she gets misty

I have seen him
cross the lawn
over there it was
right behind the third window
fump fump flumpf
you could always hear him
him & those large sensitive eyes
oh I seen him all right

& there was this way he had
once he got here
he would stand on his toes
more or less & spread
out his arms like this
& hunch over sort of

in semi-darkness this was
so there was a kind of hood
she would come in under
this was at twilight usually
when you couldn't see too good
it was all a little confused
I guess it must of bin
some kind of beach tent

anyways what would happen
she would rush in under that dark
tent affair always knew he was
coming in spirals out she'd go
fly like a filly from the starting gate
it looks like they would change right there
under night which was drizzling steadily around them

& then after awhile out they'd come
only different there's something funny now
there's been some thing happened
& there's some thing on them it's all over them
it is white so white it hurts
your eyes you can see
                there is light in their flesh

                & they leave brightpaths in the air
                     the air trembling
                          all over behind

Pluto Crat

I seen him early one night
                gargling light
want some Smithers he said
his gangly bones sprawled upon the night
sometimes when things were slow
we'd, well, we'd gargle light together, him & me
just for somethin' to do it wasn't a habit or anything ever
to tell you the truth I didn't like the taste of it, even
left a kind of sour taste, after

even worse for Dracula oh for sure
you might want to make a note of this
he had no resistance to it not a bit
not even registered light
he'd just up & guzzle like there's no tomorrow
this stuff would eat into him like rust
lay off that junk I'd tell him
it'll be the death of you sniff as sniff can

but there was no use talking to him
you could talk till yr blue in the face
it was in his blood & that was it
the guy was a terrible juicer

yeah yeah you want the story now
all right I seen him that one night
this was the last I ever set eyes on him
bubbles of light frothing from his maw
the words slippin' out like new babies
like a coyote with rabies how do i know
& that was it that was the last time

                    maybe it was an angel maybe not
                        it was so black & creaky
                        there was a flying I know

& there were these holes
as god is my witness
maybe I shouldn't say but
well there were ladies

you know   there at the edge
where the holes were, the edges, you know
he was quite the gay blade in his time

oh the holes you mean the holes
holes ok you know where things aren't
but they used to be they take things out
that's holes ok   H-O-L-E-S HOLES

& these ladies they ain't none too pleased
bein' left out or behind or beside & all
they all are beside themselves they all lean
way over into them holes squint squint
poke their fingers at the membrane of light
swear they remember Dracula
disappearing into it waving & raving
          he 's a big star now
          don't wait up he doesn't know
          when the hell will he be back
          he's on the other side
          of light now but he'll show
          when it's time
          don't worry

          & Drac Drac yr thinkin'
          I've often thought
                    the light there
    all that light in his blood   you do not want to come
it musta given him the bends
                              up again,   ever
& there he is now stuck in a nosedive

they would make funny sounds you know
what do you mean funny sounds
funny sounds you know, the ladies

do I hafta draw ya a picture fer chrissake
women make funny sounds sometimes
these women it was one of those times

                    only thing is it was kinda sad
                    they looked so desolate
        it's gettin' late & the night is pretty thin
                there among the twangly sounds
                    the balloon affair was making
                    there must a bin terrible
                    excavations in them
                    they couldn't fill
        not with all the brine in the Atlantic
not if they waited till the last molecule stopped

he takes a shine to them

                          give off steam as they do
                    they could be horses stamping winter
                              the water where it thickens
                            slush at the half-frozen holes

                        watch the streets dilate & they
                     surge the avenues my story opens
                            new venues all over town

                          up & down the lines i write
                        & now witness their whiteness
                            their red venal successions

                                    the streets shudder
                                      shut behind
                                    squirt into the book
                                      at 23 ft/sec

watch when they line up
pass in single file
past my scrutiny
my secretary of night
they must turn side
wise to get by
Nilsson says so
          & so I see
them through the lumen shine

                                              cells so red
                                          so round they are

          garnets on a necklace
                  beaded,
            in prayer

carpe diem

DNA turns into flakes walks through flesh wakes it wake
up wake up in a jerk it has been lying in dust lying in wait
flakey with desiccation DNA that curly haired bastard you
got to watch it it is so damn kinky the way it will lie to us

the twist it gives he gives to things pulls us up by the ear
tells us to dance and talk tells us to hum while we may sing
our fool hearts out for the world will soon come undressed
will come uncoiled lie in the end cold & straight & old in
the planets wild plunge

> why not then let the stars
> screw into your eyes drink
> a glass full of stars
> let our lives turn
> kinky as DNA
> will allow

a rebellion in Africa

it alarms you does it not though you mount
guard steal away all your valuables seal
your women into bedrooms into sleep
so steep they cannot gain their feet
they should be safe as the London zoo
so tight they should not move hardly dare
breathe hardly dare as it is take a breath
the stays that keep their warm bodies still

they should be safe they are in mint
condition nevertheless your mind
restless fears white from the moonlight
the way it bounces off it could be a coin
you sense night is a gland moon seeps from
fear the stars when they break out
scabbed with acne will break the seals
eat into your private store steal away
with all your valuables voluble as reds

how much you long for relief from this ache
this interminable longing this watching
for bad currency false coinage counterfeit
behind rebellions in black countries
they are after your money & your women

it terrifies you the way they rise
short of breath their eyes gone
strange the fever rises through them like Africa
they move through dreams through
rooms through windows roam by doors glide
under locks under your very look
the roar in them so loud you feel it
through your feet there are mills running
solar furnaces so close you could die

this is what you cannot handle
that they are possessed beyond you
that there is gossip in them rumours too
mysterious chemicals beyond hasps &
hinges something speeds their wrists
        click & unclick
affront you beyond bearing

it threatens to bolt past you
the ladies go out walking
at night they are getting into it
they do not steal away they leave
right in front of you past you a wide-eyed jungle
full of birds screaming their brightly coloured heads off
the look on their faces the eyes coated over
the breathing in their necks the scents they blot
they leave behind move like women sent

something in my eye

no it is nothing
you imagine
meteors falling
hail fire
works at the worlds fair
wheat in its final conflagration

nor is it emanations tumbling
stars moons planets
groaning when they pass
the sky a gigantic engine
sighs and complaints plummet from
the deepest reaches
hold you by the shoulder
push you push you toward him

no this is something
i want something
more than these wooden doors
frames wooden windows wooden picture
frames firm with nouns fastened shut
with interdiction I am tired
bearing the curt talismans the wood
crosses your hand cursing my neck

polite rosemary charms you dangle everywhere
every one of them in my room why do i think
witches screaming in fire why do i feel
my dress my collar
bone a silver necklace anointed
bloodstone my god it is
cold cold as catechism
between the perfume my breasts release
the suspicions you suspend round my neck

pale as chastity itself
it is a strange noise i can hear
 a wet tongue licking

                              my ear it is
                        cold as frog
                    a song whose words I do
                not know   but sing anyway

        it is something on my eyes
something wet & warm till I can see
where black light feeds like flies

                        a figure in red
                        a halo around him

belladonna bees

the hairs on your neck
noise away put on airs

busload of barbers
at a convention

the smell of leather & lotion
the hum of clippers

leaves crackling
all our eyes delayed

& dilating undue
lating be

latedly lighting up
something in the air some

thing warm
resin of electricity

all the bees in convection
currents stick to your neck

electric razors
covered in vaseline

give you a lot
of static those

prim & prima
donna bees

Lucy in her white body sings at night

by tongue of frog by eyes of black
frog under my tongue by earth
worms that move in knots in yellow dream
by unguent of moon I rub on my breasts
by words you whisper here on my neck
birds I have stitched round my throat
by down where your breath lies

night an enormous black
fire burning and burning
before dawn is gathered
steel wool in grass still wet
the inside of my cheek
the ache I have
scraped off my heart
press it into your hand
the days sliding off into ravines

by red fox bone I wear from my waist
by smells I scrape off wheel ruts
by bat blood I wear on my eyes
by all the water corded from the world's navel
by dove's heart marinated in moon
light my sleeping body has bathed

all the letters that burn my left hand
by nights dilation in me I call
I call you from your nails &
hammer blood come to me now
come to me now red man

in your hand the nail
that would open me

:   to you

112

he takes a lapidary interest

                              see :
              here
                        & here

          her   under the wind
          moon a   lacquer box
    one moon rises   out of water
       it could be   a salamander
          except it is   cold it is
          covered   with brine

        this is where they are wrong it is
          a hunk of wet amber this is
                Russia this is a neck
              lace on a black breast
        skin smooth so smooth the wind
        has been polishing it over & over
          its face a place insects trail
          their sticks & threads over

                    second moon an almond
                    a drift of nutmeg

        Mina herself is a moon on earth
            blood tugs from her body
        which is a kite in wind, roars silently

    from the moon menses
        flow birds gather
    night so tight it is wool
  soaked in blood it is steel
    wool shines the moon
        shines the wood
    till it is bright as bones

may the five leaves of nettle
she bears in her hand
keep her from fear & from dream

they suffer from bad circulation

have you ever listened to yourself
true you have never listened to anyone
   but why don't you for a change
try staying a wake see what happens for a change

       you in your monastic cells your communion of aints
        has it ever dawned on you how onanistic you are
        how you are into savings saving this saving that
        how much you are guided by profits preach re
      tention deposits your tightassed economy of blood
       I mean you got piles already & that's not enuff
      you gotta have more how blood-thirsty can you get
              you & your capital punishment

        you suffer from bad circulation varicose veins
bulge up your frogbelly interest muddy with blue blood
of course there is bad blood between us what do you
       expect you and your bad mouthing how you snap
        shut a purse yr lips pursed purple & prissy
          almost shout there is a terrible
            congestion you need to let go
              you & your girdled moons
           your silly & gartered persistence

you need to put things into circulation you are dying
from gangrene of the heart turned mean & gristled
need to eat my body to fortify yourselves
sooner or later you are going to eat
my words ladies & gentlemen my word
the way you feed off others their platters of blood

it can only mean one thing the mean little spirits
you hoard makes you fear inflation the red tide
the red raid when pretending to be a wall
flower you are recognized for the walking blood
bank you in truth are subject to withdrawals
overdrafts nationalization taxation the syn
tax of renewal all the purges never fear
stick with me I will save you
from yourselves dear citizens

haemophilia

                          it is a conspiracy I tell you
                   yes a breathing together that too you &
                          your bad breath the garlic on
vector: an animal that transmits a
    disease-producing organism from one host to
    another
                                    it will be the death of us
                            though you deny it
                            the evidence is plain
                            you want me removed
                   from circulation the small elation
                                    you feel in that
            thot how you form networks with your nerves
            so you can block my word with old blood
            lines spread your colicy & invalid words across
            passage after passage blocked out in streets
vector: a physical quantity with both magnitude
    and direction such as force or velocity

            sometimes they are spider cables meant to slice
            my thoughts off slick as Robespierre
            your cheese-cutter nerves your
            unaired lives choked in distemper

most often they are fibrous bandages across the wounds
they trap platelets & corpuscles trap breath
such a barricade of blood till you cannot

what Lucy speaks to me you cannot
stop cannot hear there
they are Lucy's bright
words bright with oxygen
let loose they are
lucid with love my own
worlds muffled in the criss
crosses the double crosses you would
cross me out though you do not
know in all these crossings the crossings
over crossings up the cross sings
her replies no longer trapped
Luce if her words mean anything

oh no when I call to her i call
bold bud pet bed pat spit bad i call
dab apt rub dip tip pit bid bird part
my labials my dentals my sliders

ruddy as a ruby
throated humming
bird i am singing
from her throat
loud as glucose

money talks

pop   pop   pop you say

i say my deah

deah boy

fruity voices you prefer to call cultivated

                            all i want is you
                   there you stand at the doorway
                spatula in hand that you dracula
        better wash up real quick suppers gettin cold

well no not that that's not it not quite
but i hadja for a minute there dint i
c'mon admit it you were sucked in
                     just a little

anyways i get, well, a little pissed
          off i guess yd say
when you squirt tasteful little shotguns
onto the newsprint the talk you shoot into cable cars
real big shot this is
a showdown & you your are really smoking
loges cloud up with your baggy & boring speeches
bulge with god & wives & good god gold, money
there it goes in big & huffy puffs
big money we're talkin here
cash bills cheques lines of credit vouchers
cartoons balloon with your many manly talks
lets face it money talks
suspended in the bubbles
you emit ceremoniously parsimoniously
from your purple & pursed lips
pursuit pursuit you cry prissy as all get out

you blow & they harden, the bubbles,
    preserve you &
your class in your glass
cases your tinctured musings
silly as the monocles you wear
on your faces clear evidence in any case
hard to know what to do or say

when entire streets are filling in with talk
it could be one big potato bin, the street
your speeches press squeakily together
sticky as hate on the walls & ceiling

no end to your shovey speeches
moustachey talk that's what it is
what you cant stand you hate to see
me a big pop star & all
doesn't know his place
blasting with shrapnel your stuffy talk
                              sweepin in here prickin
                              the little bags of bombast
                              you keep flying
                              off & fooling people
hoping for a big return

a lightness that rises

a lightness that rises
    moons quick flight
   the phosphorous faces
   bones fused & burning
the landscape of your skin
    touches the bruises
  the hot white moons
  all night long roll
       so sharply focussed you can see
       clouds thudding into the hills
       louder than shovels

everything in its throes every night
the neon of birds their nearness
stars in their brains your bones
the dark yawns in its throat

sd the smell of semen perfumed the room
& birds their quick snap of syn
tax every morning at breakfast they break
open & shut, nevada tickets, sentences they write
break & shut break & shut so fast
the shutter seems fluent
sometimes silent sometimes shaken
as if they were wood whose flight stuck

under skin the whole world an apartment
& we in saline suspended
each body a valise filled with ultraviolet
the violence with which
its bright currency rubs off

birds are eating our eyes the sky
rusting the whole universe
seizing earth a sickening sound
running out of music
            out of time

black angel

you with your broken mouth
hold me bent
at the throat like a wish
bone you will not let go till I bless you
you say you would die if I left you you say
you do not care about gossip
you want something from me
shake me so much i cld be a broken wagon
a missing father you clutch
tighter than a child her doll
you give it a good talking to
a damn good shaking

is it that I fly? bite? remove
nails from wood? hang from
nails in your wormwood dreams? do you
want the name?
of my orthodontist? what do you think
of mews? a redwinged blackbird?
is this what you want from me?

Don't you know from time
to time I must return die again
& again blood squirting from me
a ruptured fire hose
a torn & mangled corpse

I know though you shudder
you want & claim
will not be denied
your pound of flesh
your pint of blood

you hop right to it
red-breasted with blood
lap it up and hope for more
you want to be there
on the cutting edge don't you

know anything don't you
know though you would prefer it
if I were a bottled frog mottled blue
    & bug-eyed old roue safe
in a canister set rubbery as an old safe
filled to overflowing with formaldehyde

well you got your hands
               full with me
relative or no relative you got more
than you bargained for far
more than you deserve

        I am not only the exquisite kite you know
        you take me for the one which flies
        under slides through air pulls
        a cord undoes blue thunder

            think of me then when you do
             think of me as a great blue
              heron hooked on your neck
                right out of the blue
               hangar a flying thing
              hung up on my hunger
              sold on your blue vein
           your exquisite blue vanity
              stored in the closet

        staring in the window
       stutter of hail at the pane

I will go I will
do I know not what
it is or comes for
only that it finds me
my emily heat, the strewn night

hits hard as sunstroke
cold muscle thuds
my own heart sudden
as doorslam
thuds & thuds & thuds
till I think   I must die

the whole world whirls
& whirls &
&
then   all at once
every
thing
stops—

the red
emption of blood

sure i am
they're right
i am
a burglar of blood
bugler of salivation the seventh seal busted
there can be no X
emption
before the distant & indistinct roar

come as doctor, would relieve the pressure
a little loyal bleeding, it's good for the realm

you should spend some time on me
to redeem currency it is a holy thing I do
these transactions withdrawals from
the banks the sepulchres your bodies
have become

would take things into my own hands
break open what is
within you to give , tithing

broadcast in a barren land
bright coins of your blood

you snap night open

like a pea the intense feeding & drinking you know that
my life depends on you i wld freeze, dry up
turn into a mummy blow away my god good people
without me what would become of you
without you i am nothing my blood goes
sluggish as water in winter
wells to my finger tips yours too
puffy with want

                         when there is no S
                 caping the thumbs i gasp you grasp
           a leather jacket suitcase
                 you snap open night
         cant breathe
                   its welts
      the sudden wet rips
              /open
      the fingersmooth bodice
     the unripeness that falls
             beautiful as bank notes you wld say
         shock of your white bodies pealed
                 revealed to themselves

     im pale too see what you
    impale me on
  your beauty
         fast leap of it all

ventriloquist

i warm to you
you & your necrophilia
step into your traffic
light shivers, leaps
a lark leaks out
your armour
your blood blinking
stop stop

you are grateful amazed
you are enamoured
the way i charm
embroider the borders
your bodies brood on

carnelian garnet agate
on the lives you enamel
& forget

on the underside of your love
i throw my love
around your neck throw
away all hands & gloves
i am clearly indelible

face it my lady from here on in
i am on
& i won't
come off

dangerous liaisons

Fllu-UMm ᴾᴾ spread my hand my life
fast like that like gasoline on fire
its long wires & membranes are moist
daedalus diving for all hes for
gotten & gone dead in
old daedalus driving
       me to you to me to you
          .my hand   .my life
   spread before you
               come in

   see this is my shade
shed for you my pain & umbre
come in my lady you can see
couched how painterly i am
i can see it in your eyes say
    its not right this sudden
wind this cool lust on the wind
   thick as licorice once more

you want to get off the hook do you not
                 no do not
take umbrage in your rage at your age
lady in rouge you should thank me think of me
umbilicus from dreams past
    glories you are lost upon & must
  drink from again past age surely
naked as stones in pastures devout
as inincunabulus i implore you

the moon & stars passing through

a garden of stones they dream under
scabby & prickled lives, now puddles
now pickles the vinegar moon secretes

room after room of bones
we have all taken rooms
it is plain someone has
tucked us in for eons

all the bones since the beginning of time
time has sewn inside earth
earth turns faster & faster on its pain
the bones the wounds fester
until one day the bones are thrown

out again & again the face of earth will laugh
all the bones will fling into music
boxes bird bones cow bones turtle bones
giant lizard bones fish bones people bones
everywhere the beautiful bones
the centrifuge centuries have spun

all night long we rhyme
our bones click
winds fizz
it is the moon & the stars
passing through
in slurs & whizzes
all day long going black

going back east this is how we tell time
in seed time it is clusters tumbling
harvest time too the restless skies
seething angels endlessly rolling
round the sky like wine barrels
fish in our talk   thought   sleep
sometimes quick sometimes thick

the sounds from lights on a marquee
sounds of insects flashing
announcing the coming and fatal attraction
the zuzz you feel in your teeth & worry
will they crack when your flannel
memories sleep with the bones
time has cleared of waiting

                    it is not what you think
        we are more lovely
than sullen we are entangled with stars
rattle to one another for centuries
wonder where has all our flesh gone
when in the empty dormitory of dream
    will we ever again pick it up
bring our flesh together feel it packed
                    in wedges
sweet spasm of life

                stars as ever inconstant
        our thoughts their chalk
when we talk at the blackboard
sounds of fingernails when the black is
                        pulled down
        slams shut around us

hors d'oeuvres

he had these new fangled jaws
he could be a can opener

jaws of death he called them
& he yawned, or pretended

this is when he pries night open with them
tears it open with a ripping sound
& it gurgles & thrashes

streets filled with olives & sardines
he opens every night
serves them up on the canape
he takes out of the sky
dilettante the way he folds
things & bites them
in a tasteful manner

except what was really funny was
he had a real knack as lip reader
could sense through the deepest fog
the wet red lips what they were saying

he would go straight for the nearest larynx
played it like a bagpipe
like wind down a chimney
chummy as a border collie at supper

in which he makes espousals

know that we are confirmed
in catastrophes of blood

  each to other
  earth to east we are
  confirmed and find ourselves
     with & in one

   another me
  the angel of dispersal
  have heard the wonder
     full logohhrea
  & said
I will follow you to & fro
   to the ends

    so construed I
   weep at your collar
     red fox
   stole to your passions

    thief of love
   here in manitoba
   where the wind
   itself comes un
   housed & the red
    river flows

 my face looms
big as a boulder

 you yourself should be a little bolder
 you should give me my head

the inspector interviews

Yes yes I saw that man,
the one you are looking for.

Well, it's hard to say how, exactly.
There was a smell, burnt lilacs sort of,
from behind the dray,
            and then him.

Well not that exactly, I mean
he didn't just show up suddenly, or something.
What happened was there was a
huge bread basket he sort of
            fell out of, like.

Where was this exactly?

The sky. It was in the sky.

It was orange, solid orange,
and the sky, that's where.

And he fell out?

        fell out, plop
    —like bread dough.
What's the matter? You don't listen too good?

Bread dough?

Yeah, bread dough. What you think
they keep in the bread basket, vinegar?

Ok, fine.   Can you describe him?

Yeah.

So?

You sure you're the inspector?

Ok, what'd he look like?

Well why didn't you say so, that part's easy, that's why I
called. Didn't they tell you?

Well?

so

well . . .   the flowers

what

so   you said so

Oh yes he was such a dashing man, such a handsome devil
he should be on stage, my goodness, so tall and dark
and that smile of his, my oh my.

The flowers?

Oh yeah sure, I was comin'   to the flowers.
That's what it is see, that's the   important part. I mean
can   you imagine it's steaming cold midnight, not even
a cat's shown a whisker tonight, talk   about lonely,
streets empty like   that, you could hear   the flowers
growing, this   yellow vapour drifting drifting   you can
hear the men way cross the river at   the dock.

the flowers

They're talkin away, voices over water, wet on your
face, and then there it is, not a sound.

what   what

a sound

Mostly you get sound, bock bock
bock, feet on stone, you know, a sound you said a sound,
or wood, when it's been around, but this time—nothing.
Not a tick. And then I see it—this big bunch of red
flowers, a fistful of the reddest flowers you ever seen,
mister.

yes

this man.

what   what man
hhnmnm
what about him you mentioned a man
          Yes. Of course I did. He was right there.
Where?
          there. right there.   there
               Behind the flowers. This handsome fellow.
          What about the fellow?

          Well he just trailed behind, mostly,
like smoke, didn't he, only there is no shadow,
after? there he was a fistful of strings & he's
holdin on tight and won't let go dancin' sort of,
under it, legs loose spaghetti. look lady . . . . this
big handful of flowers only they are hearts and he
is floating from them and he yells hay Mona up
here what what yeah up here wanna lift and I ran
coz I did I did only what they dripped all over me
and he was gone flowers and all

so you don't have to bite my head off just becoz.

136

finders keepers

what you say in your watery & warty soul
the tight-lipped rectitute you sit on
rocks could not parachute through
would wreck like falling stars
your body an iron grate
    in the assizes of your days
    you cannot hear the systole or diastole
    under your dazed months your mouth tight
    thumb tacks stuck chastely in blue
        velvet, chastizing

say you are into retention into keeping
house keeping mum your mouth shut
your morals up morals imperative
mere mortals tell me
I can bank on that

    it has gone to your head madam
    bloodless as a cantaloupe
    & it keeps us from ourselves

    why can't we just up & elope I say
    give over to ourselves our heads
    dangling we could run
    away bounce over macadam roads
    every thing in us a swishing
    wishing, thick as lemmings, as fast

this is why I follow my head
why I hang on your word
dangle by the neck at your neck
our bodies share seek to shave off
the withholding removal retraction
place settings walnut clocks the sugar box egg stand
every housely every rehearsed gesture of rectitude

he comes to the back

no i am not
what you believe
you see

an elegant aristocrat
cool & perfect
as a new cut
decanter a black
& polished shoe

all this is invalid
what you don't see
when you see me is

the red meat
shambling
the alleys you vacate
all the edicts your evictions
my dreams rubbed raw
their cold shumbling

though i do embroider
your throat with red thread
you must see
the utter need
i am a raw stomach
ulcerous for love

am a stutter at the gate
crushed grape where
they step, disregarding
you a wet flower gape at
shudder the back
step i stop stoop perplexed at

that's me dear people
a sack it soaks through

heave myself onto your porch
dependence of a shaggy beast
        though you see only
the mute scream a snake makes

                shoulders banging at doors
                like cymbals escaped moons
                hoping some one will
                    take me in
                i am an invalid
                        please
                    take me
                        in

139

forget it

forget it
you won't let him
off the hook

it's all a lie
you don't want
to feel it anymore
when you close
your eyes the braille
barely audible at the tips
your fingers the feeling
in them almost gone
when you crawl under
the covers you are
being blinded
slightly when i turn
on the lights
& let him go

the end

when at last you turn
         at the back
door you will put him
back close the lid on his face
a jar of preserves of some kind
only he will leave
        a mark faintly
   embossed pattern
            a dint in water
             smudge of winter
    water mark in march

         don't you want to keep
         in touch you plead
         thrilled with what has happened
         please write drop me
         a line sometime
         drop in sometime \ really
                              it's been great